T0193147

Deviant Propulsion
CAConrad

soft skull press

Deviant Propulsion: Poems
ISBN: 1-932360-87-5
Copyright © CAConrad, 2006

Cover photograph of CAConrad © Greg Fuchs, 2006.
www.gregfuchs.com

Cover & interior design: Alexandra Escamilla

Published by Soft Skull Press
55 Washington Street
Suite 804
Brooklyn, NY 11201
www.softskull.com

Distributed by Publishers Group West
www.pgw.com | 800.788.3123

Library of Congress Cataloging-in-Publication Data

Conrad, C. A.
  Deviant propulsions : poems / by C.A. Conrad.
      p. cm.
  ISBN-13: 978-1-932360-87-5 (alk. paper)
  1. Marginality, Social--Poetry. 2. Working class--Poetry. 3. Gays--Poetry. I.
Title.

PS3603.O555D48 2005
811'.54--dc22
                                                        2005001054

Acknowledgments

The author gratefully acknowledges the editors of the following magazines, where some of these poems first appeared: *AboutPoetry.com, Accent, Ambit, American Writing, Amethyst, canwehaveourballback?, Chiron Review, Columbia Poetry Review, CrossConnect, Dusie, Exquisite Corpse, Gayety,* the *Hat, Highway Robbery, Iris, Joss, La Petite Zine, Lilliput Review, LIT, Lodestar Quarterly, Mad Poets Review, M.A.G.,* the *New Guard, One Shot, Oyster Boy Review, Pearl, Philadelphia Independent, Poetry Broadside, Poetry Motel, POeP!, Pom2, Powhatten Review, Range, Real Poetik, Shrike, Transcendental Visions,* and *VeRT.*

"R.S.V.P." won first place in the *Chiron Review* Poetry Contest.

"In the Black Forest before the Birth of Rilke" appeared in the anthology *Thus Spake the Corpse: An Exquisite Corpse Reader* (Black Sparrow).

"P for Interest in Waking" appeared in the anthology *26 Letters, 26 Poets: An Anthology of Poems Commissioned in Celebration of the Rosenbach Museum & Library's Exhibition R Is for Rosenbach* (Pew Fellowships in the Arts).

"Torn Ligament Chorephilia for Marwan" and "Subterrestrial Aria for Kevin Killian and Dodie Bellamy" appeared in the *DC Poetry Anthology* (DC online).

"A World without Condoms" and "Deviant Propulsion" appeared in the documentary *The Poetry Project,* filmed and directed by Greg Fuchs.

"evaporate again" was a chapbook (Mooncalf Press).

"Exit as Real Journey to All Friends" was a chapbook (Furniture Press).

"POETS REFINE MONEY" appeared as a limited-edition broadside (Half Empty/Half Full Press).

Special thanks to Shanna Compton for her expert advice. (www.shannacompton.com)

dedicated to
Marsha P. Johnson
Maryse Holder
Jackie Curtis
and all other
deviant
shit-kickers!
*much thanks
to you!*

Contents

"Those who restrain desire, do so
because theirs is weak enough
to be restrained."
—William Blake

"Poetry *IS*
independent
media!"
—Frank Sherlock

```
            for    years
            they waited
            in     their
            j u n g l e s
for         canned           ham
peanut          butter       30
second          burgers      it's
true            it's         true
            wrap   any
            one    you
            want   in
            t  o  r  n
            atlas  my
            a m e r ic a
            a    million
            p o s s i b l e
            w o r l d s
            but       we
            c h o o s e
            to     feed
            the    rich
```

Dear Mr. President There Was Egg Shell under Your Desk Last Night in My Dream!

Dear Mr. President this morning i called my cousin in Wyoming his boyfriend was making the coffee like many good people do in this beautiful country my cousin told me to tell you it's madness you bring us when i told him i was writing to you today it's been awhile since i've seen you in person on the streets of Philadelphia you were waving and then you were speaking hey we've all heard the stories of your cocaine and booze and i want to say i'm sorry about your parents i'm sure other children of CIA brass need a little craziness to get a little loose do a line of coke get naked and run around campus were you freer back then of course you were i'm an idiot for asking and i remember cologne when you spoke in Philadelphia and i know it was your cologne you had that i'm-wearing-cologne air about you see i believe there's a big man inside you and yes we're angry right now yes it's about war yes it's about many things the things men with little time for love will impose on others and i wish i could say HEY we're all going to be dead in a hundred years so let's shift the pace let's forget about war let's pass a Let's Get Naked and Crazy National Holiday i wish it was this easy but nothing is ever easy with a man who has little time for love and a man with little time for love is really just a man who hasn't had love yet you haven't really had love yet there's no way you could have had love real love and not want every human body to have medical care if they need it have education if they want it have more time with their families and loves like we all NEED it Mr. President i'm worried your self-esteem was damaged many years ago and keeps you from seeing us out here our bodies our black and white and red and yellow and Iraqi and Korean bodies and we're all a little fucked-up with our problems but i know i JUST know there's a big

2

man inside of you big enough to really SEE need and offer without hesitation because you can because there is plenty you are stronger than your father's blueprints for your life i've seen your fingers in person you have nice hands Mr. President and they're your hands not your father's hands your life is your own it really is it belongs to you and love is waiting i have a lot of love Mr. President and i just want to press against you sometimes to let you get a little of it HEY i'm so serious about this let's go away together this spring just the two of us it's not a big deal don't even tell anybody i mean you're the president after all but there's a marvelous stretch of woods where i grew up we could smoke a little pot to wind you down get you out of your oval office mode maybe a little wine i'm sure you need a good massage maybe we could go to the creek and paint secret mud symbols on our naked bodies like i used to do with my first boyfriend what happens after that will be fine you'll see it will be okay the break in the woods has the best flowers to rest beside in the sun and you will awaken with a crown of honeysuckle beautiful man that you are a real leader of real lives who can change the world

with real love waiting for you
CAConrad

the   only
f a i l u r e
i s   n o
l   o   v   e
wait   for
me   wait
for   us
p l e n t y
P L ENTY
e v e r y
b o d y ' s
t i c k e t
will   be
t   o   r   n
wine   and
a p p l e s
warm our
a r d e n t
p u l s e
l   o   v   e
i s   f o r
the   pretty
AND THE
R E S T
OF   US
his   naked
b o d y
q u i e t s
b o m b e r
e n g i n e s
i   a m
g l i d i n g
f r o m

some mornings your hair is EXACTLY the way you want it when you wake up and you don't shower to not mess it and you want the trees of Philadelphia to smell EXACTLY who you are sweat and semen of your lover MY GOD IT'S BEAUTIFUL OUT HERE it feels good until it feels superficial then you feel guilty and if you are lucky you stop...understand guilt as someone else's idea AND YOU GET THE love again

i'm falling in love
aimlessly
it's nice

i think i won something
but i'm not sure

i always think
i'm winning things that
aren't there

Marwan fucks
me in the front
seat of his
taxi cab which
isn't easy in
Philadelphia while
making a turn onto
Benjamin Franklin
Parkway at 3 a.m.

it's Daylight
Savings Time i'm
angry i'm losing
an hour

he says "tomorrow is
April Fool's Day
ask me to do
something we'll
both enjoy"

i ask him
to back
his ass onto
the gear shift
until it feels
good and
he does

Deviant Propulsion

"to be mindlessly in flower
past understanding"
—Jonathan Williams

Robert Creeley cab
driver look
alike or maybe
because we
just left
City Lights
Bookstore

how many
Chinatown
ducks did
Kerouac eat?
a total?
okay, an
estimate

"i don't know"
Magdalena says
"but nothing's
better than a
pretty girl's
sphincter!"

Buddhist monk
on cell phone
i point
to hear
her mutter
"Postmodern" again

she won't
drive down
Bush Street
because of the
president not
the genitalia

"i want to
rub my titties
all over this
city!" she says

"me too!" i say
today's inner child
a sexy old whore

if he/she has
a cock i'll
ask him/her
for a dance
"but if there's
pussy down
there get
out of
my way!"
Magdalena roars

may the best
genitals win!
i'm a faggot
competing with
a dyke for a
piece of ass
someone mutter
"Postmodern" please

where'd you
first hear
your meat
curtain slang?
all those
vaginal
synonyms
hip for
Scrabble to
flip her
switch up

then she
drove to the
hotel of
her first
lesbian sex
only she
couldn't
find it
i mean the
hotel and
the traffic
cop made
us go
thru a
tunnel our
living
metaphor in
motion

You Not as Me but You

*"The two most common lies men
have told me are, 'the check is in
the mail' and 'I promise not to
cum in your mouth.'"*

—my mother

orphan light
does not
exist
just the thought
just as though
running had
a chance we
die living or
live dying

imagine
forgetting to
invent
washing
machines but
we make
it to Mars

we would've
invented
disposable
clothes instead

sacrifices for
new edges

theory of
avalanche
falls out of
head
crashes into
others

for anger's
sake it
enters us
exiting
wrong

when were
there so
many i
couldn't
see you?

can i
always
see you
now?
please?

my cock follows
my pussy-sized
heart happy
someone invented
your candy ass

how did
you get so
delicious?

your mother
thought i thanked
her for the
food when i
thanked
her for
the food

look at this
Gideon's Bible
do they really
think people
in hotels
are lonely?

not in
these
cheap
rooms

thinning the
walls of
sanity

translucent

it's
turning
into
amnesia for
patience

my mother
warned me
men will
shit on
Love

"no-no
you're
wrong" you say
"your mother
warned you
not to BE
the man who
shits on Love"

oh yeah,
thanks

Torn Ligament
Chorephilia
for Marwan

he takes
himself from
the dance
has not
seen how
i see
every
step

the table holds
appointments of
sugar
bread
fingers his
semen will
fertilize
nothing
in me

but i
take it

run it
on edges
of bills
magically
paid

while
rain lets
me lift
my stem
i'd rather
burst than
bloom
so…

it is
just
so

the diver
pitched into
nothing more
than a
tub
spiders make
a few
walls
home

but i want
to be a
prairie dog in
the apartment
poke from
floors
greet my
neighbors

hold the
book warm
from his
hands
put it
back before
he comes
from the
toilet

it's when
a poem
closes in
the oven

you can
not see a
different view
from the
window if
it is a
painting
(but every
now and
then…)

———————

carry another
sex on your sex
in your fellow
human streets
look and look
listen listen
this risen
spirit

trying hard
to belong
to no one

hail down
the want!

STOP making
maps for
those
wanderers!

step from
a giant
ass fully
clothed

another week
in the trash with
alarming speed

our sudden
death our
shittiest
surprise

"what's fair?" we
asked once

"never heard of it"
our answer arrived
no return address

what's the big deal with sex in poeMs i Mean really are
you poet or pontiff sex of antenna knee caps all our
Mothers and fathers driving to factories and offices
listening to jaMes brown with jittery knees is a Marvelous
thing is positively breathtaking jaMes brown true father
of us all Making our parents wet and hard and you say
sex in poeMs is self indulgent well i'M not interested in
writing soMething to spite you but i love sex all hail
another generable gene probe have soMe fucking faith
you tight asses get the genie of genital vibrancy My
grandMother played the auto harp to tug My grandfather
naked and i'M here to praise it the vicar of christ hiMself
couldn't shout loud enough oh coMe on now let those
priests and nuns have a go at life so they stop buggering
your children fish net stockings and babylonian lube stick
hell has a lovely little theMe song kind of catchy in true
victory colors while your abstinence is iMpertinence
righteous alMighty i Mean elvis stabbed the air with his
fucking pelvis for decades to set your ass free darling yet
it's still so naughty naughty naughty with your Mighty
iMperforations despite honeycreeper honeyeater
honeydew delirious why else the word honey in
honeyMoon you Moron unzip and let it fly celery viagra
alMonds roasted cherries hashish kaMa sutra coca cola
spanish fly the phallic shaped hookah My Mother bought
at the pawn shop fed My eyes and taste buds the Musical
nutrition of being coMpletely alive sex the closest we get
to source don't be hoodwinked into shadows i'd put sex
in every single poeM if it were not for My absolute fear of
Monotony

M

M loves M carved on sycamore
M found tied and gagged by jealous P and O
M portrait in my locket
M more hump than N
M orders I into fan blade
M crossbow shoots Y off planet
M full of banjo strings serenades U
M scratched inside Melville's coffin lid
M Michelangelo chiseled into David
M Frank O'Hara beautiful without one
M Freddie Mercury Rest in Peace
M on Mormon Funeral Home silverware
M hovers on blackboard

M is its sound
M two mountains with valley
M two waves with submarine you can't see
M two tee pees winter alone on paper
M three fingers pointed down
M sideways someone's beak
M means 6 to telephones
M 50,779 listings in Philadelphia's Directory
M middle initial my neighbor won't explain
M Yukio Mishima's big one and little one
M Lady Macbeth's big one sharpens knives
M Marilyn Monroe's two big false ones
M written on thighs with honey

M branding irons
M ice cubes hide in puddles
M noodle soup
M parachutes into bra conventions
M around camel humps
M around toes
M around testicles
M ankle cuffs
M naughty for the shy
M and S
M new crucifix design
M my answer to your every interrogation
M used 67 times in this poem

In the Black Forest
before the Birth of Rilke

under her skirts of bark
the hidden pencils grow

———————

legs do
it all
head bobbing
a free ride

it's no
telephone she
holds a dying
bird to her
ear as legs
get them
there the
whispered
names of
you 'n' me

It Really Was for Love

one day we
said let's
replicate
flowers
and not
buy real
ones any
more

It's True I Tell Ya
My Father Is a 50¢
Party Balloon

my father paper thin again
lost on the basement floor

but who will put their lips
to his stiff old hard-on?
who will blow him up?
who will want this
man floating
stupid
stuck in
a tree again?

A World without Condoms

she swears it was the cucumber

nine months later
a son with
her eyes and
cheekbones
but the seeded spine and
leafy complexion are all Dad's

the nurse rubs a little Creamy Italian
on his bright green belly
they coo at one another
blow bubbles at one another
"this won't hurt a bit" she says
and tucks the napkin
under her chin

Crows, beautiful murder of crows along the highway. More than anything my beautiful black brothers I want to pull over, bear a child, for you, crows, eat my baby, eat him, pick his baby eyes, he's for you brothers, eat him, ah, sweet murder of crows, eat him before he can ask your names.

———————

suppose you are
airtight—in an egg—and you feel "ready"
though your panel of instruments
reads UNSAFE CONDITIONS BEYOND
        THE CALCIUM CRUST!
this is the story i'm beginning to tell you

departures at
2 a.m. not
midnight

my imaginary bus
turns into a plate
of spaghetti in
Howard Johnson on
Times Square

4th booth from
the register reading
a poet who
liked Chaucer but i
don't have to like
Chaucer to like this
poet i'm not
saying i don't
like Chaucer
i'm just saying

meanwhile
the men who filed down
Times Square's edges
enter the hearth

The Distance

all the
death has a
way of
getting us
the love

it's always
what's
missing from
anything that's
missing

one tries
to extend love
by trying to
distend for love

salutes you back

it's not
philosophy it's
a kiss moving
down your
spine

it holds

one day you
can't believe
how much
it holds

nobody
cares because
you're not
in the
movies

a roof
allows a
house
underneath

the can
calls out
for the
can opener
as much
as the
peas
tragically
inside i'm
talking about
love still

you were
wild for
someone in
the distance
but it
was a
mirror

Imbibe

I've never played
violin never touched
one till now
   how did I convince
them my god the place
is packed balconies even
   I walk out how am
I doing
   (applause applause)
I could run off
I could tell them
I could stare laugh
   cry fall over
I could faint
   "Violinist faints
every evening and
Sunday matinees"

how do you die when
you really need to

instead
I lift my bow
play Vivaldi
and wonder how it is
I came to surrender

went to the
Eileen Myles
New York
book party
with Hassen

massive heart attendance
hold my purse i'm
about to d

        rop
something in
       the sky

first
bird flew
like no
one
saw

Ah over Om
our last pack
of headless
riders

never wrong
reminding
them of
freedom never
never never
wrong

if Eileen made
a kite which
poem would
she choose?

POETS REFINE MONEY

There are thousands of Americans everyday who are looking for a safe place to invest their money. Poets are the best source for removing negative charge from your wealth, and raising the collective conscience of the planet. You can change your life FOREVER by sponsoring a poet today! CAConrad is one such American poet serious about making poetry a lifelong quest, ready and willing to refine your money! If you are interested in sponsoring this poet, call (215)563-3075, or write to CAConrad13@AOL.com. You won't believe the difference a poet will make!

as though none
of us exist he
reads only
dead poets

those frigid
necropoetics

can he
feel these
contradictions
of light falling
around us?

it's my poet
genius friends
who excite
me to
write

checking
with the
music in
my head

i go to
them
aspirin
melting
in hand
running
thru the
rain

Exit as Real Journey
to All Friends

"I am looking for the face I had
Before the world was made."
—W.B. Yeats

loneliness keeps
total order or
none at all

sitting
in box
pulling
levers at the
speed of
dreams

follow
trail of
bubbles
down
where
child you
cannot recreate
stays
there

staying alive
poetry's only
necessary
purification

Love,
from the strange
steel of the earth

mother's
tax-free
shoplifting always
nutritious always
delicious

mmM, and mr.
president we are
not confused
military assistance be
military assault

to
believe
anyone but
the rich
are the
enemy

taker
wins all

cruelty's
madness first
a hunger

gone tilting
on a sad beach

reaching for
poets who
reach back

who gave
Love the
heart? fuck
the heart
i Love you
with all
my liver

not knowledge
but stupidity
wakes the
tough
student

because
liver
can't
do the
job!

tilting sad
on a gone beach

imaginary
or not
let's
cross the
line
together
friend

we are
dirt
don't
worry turn us
inside out

lemon slice
too small to
remember
the tree

growls
from
mirror
resemble
mother

open the
sleep they
mail us

pleased and
open

poem
lowering
from
air where
air gives

"we
must be
up inside
the cyclone"
so says Dorothy
engine's
large ingestion
of birds

compass not
working in
outer space
where
endless
mazes home are
some stories

click of
astronaut's
helmut wakes
us confused

day will
come we'll
need the
page we
ripped
away

scrubbing
stain to
never miss
it later

you are
the first
i'd call if
poetry didn't
exist

battering
walls of
flesh the
heart

Subterrestrial Aria for
Kevin Killian &
Dodie Bellamy: 1st Watch

in Philadelphia
when donut
shops turn
to porn only
Believers
belong to
karma and
then
as before
the rest
of us
are free

Magdalena says
to say i'm
financially
secure means
i'm okay
being poor

and need
no understanding

the one
with good
eyes points
from windows
to the flare
of suicide
42 bombers

the rapist's
therapists
embroider
small thoughts
on couches in
documentaries
ending for some
reason when
threads pull
back into
accordion
cases animals
died to cover

every suffering
thing makes
its way into
us soon enough

imagine tasting
wind through
fields of
wheat in
bread

let's build
balconies in
the cellar
where we
toast friendship
lighting root
of lilac
and oak
worms and
moles our
nightingales
of mud and
quartz
the world is
ending they say
but yesterday
shushed
a buzz

today the
new world

poem you
Armageddon
bullhorn
wake us
every
street the
free ones

Subterrestrial Aria for
Kevin Killian &
Dodie Bellamy: 2nd Watch

it's really fine
here they say

after 2 or 3 miles
we realize we're
driving in
Cy Twombly's
paintings

it's really fine
here though

our ladder makes
an appearance
rung of rabbit
rung of wolf
broken rung of
darkskin wrapped
in flames of cash

i want some
orange juice
i want some
burgers

changing face
of Hector with
Achilles our
exit sign
baseball bats
pounding
gravity
out of
the car

wishing

we were

on ground

again

wish you
had invited
me to your
poetry
reading instead of
your wedding

there's no
where for me
to hide my
feelings of
optimal sugar *all of a sudden!*

all right
i give up!
(unexpected instant
applause in my
head for surrendering
very frightening)

My Mother after
Knee Surgery

she calls it her
new knee it's in
everything she
says her
new knee

hide my book of
poems tired of
explaining

she distracts herself
with television
i watch to
share her
concentration
into
dis—sss—sstance

when it's boring
she makes herself
a drink
pours
me one

drink gets
television
interesting

"hey, remember when i was
a kid i asked why humans
aren't extinct, and you said
it's because we're afraid
of the dark?"

"bullshit, hey, c'mon now,
i'm trying to relax my
new knee dammit!"

14 Conversations

ME: I love the smell of laundromats in strange cities.

CITY: Define strange.

ME: (shocked to hear from city and can answer nothing).

◎◎◎◎

ME WITH HAT: Everything seems so uncertain now.

ME WITHOUT HAT: Things were certain at one time?

ME WITH HAT: Well yes, but after what happened, now things are uncertain.

ME WITHOUT HAT: If things were certain how could you be surprised by what happened?

◎◎◎◎

HER: (extending clipboard) Would you like to sign our petition to help end deforestation?

ME: I'd like to, but I work in a bookstore, it's a holocaust for trees.

◎◎◎◎

SHE: (hands my poem back to me) Why don't you write
　　something happier?

ME: How's it possible to deny one unhappiness as well!?

◎◎◎◎

ME: I want dress in a bishop's robe and bless rush hour
　　traffic with one hand, with a sign in the other
　　"IGNORE THIS BLESSING YOU HAVE ALL YOU
　　NEED!"

MICHELLE: Can you be arrested for impersonating a holy man?

ME: But we're all holy.

◎◎◎◎

ME: I want to STORM an easter egg hunt, invoke some
　　crazy ancient pagan sniffing under trees for dinner.

CANDACE: Yeah man, that's cool! I want to combine easter with
　　4th of July and have red, white and blue
　　EXPLODING CRUCIFIXES!

◎◎◎◎

ME: HEY! Did you turn my friends into pigs!?

CIRCE: Honey, they were pigs already, I'm trying to turn
　　them into men.

ME: Oh. Okay, gee, thanks.

◎◎◎◎

ME: I love that we have the sky. Do you love that we have the sky?

ADRIANNE: But think about how much closer the clouds could be.

◎◎◎◎

ME: Mmmm! Mm! God! This is so good!

MOM: Mmmmm, Mm Hm, yeah. That's because it's stolen.

ME: Why is it so delicious because it's stolen?

MOM: Mmmm. Because I only steal gourmet.

◎◎◎◎

MARWAN: (wearing turquoise shoes disguised as purple) Have you ever smelled a crematorium?

ME: (wearing turquoise shoes disguised as black) Sure, are you kidding, this is Philadelphia, I walk past steak shops everyday, oxygen incorporates scorched flesh.

◎◎◎◎

ME WITH
EYES OPEN: In nature, wild buffalo leave the weak to die.

ME WITH
EYES CLOSED: But this is a grocery store, why can't I see?

◎◎◎◎

MAN WITH
CLIPBOARD: Would you please sign our petition to save dolphins
caught in tuna nets?

ME: If I sign, does it mean I don't care about the tuna?

ⓞⓞⓞⓞ

HIM: It's amazing it doesn't have buds yet.

HER: But it's not a plant, it's a duck.

HIM: One does not have to be a plant to have flowers!
Just look at ME! (tears open shirt to reveal perfect
blisters of marigold and zinnia)

DUCK: Quack, quack!

HIM: Hmmm, quite nice that flower's song.

ⓞⓞⓞⓞ

SALESMAN: Would you be interested in hearing rates for our new
life insurance policy?

ME: I have a recycling plan, code name Kublah Kahn.

SALESMAN: Pardon me?

ME: Too many crucifixes to focus at once.

P for Interest in Waking

Pertho East)))))))))
bigger than an ant only in size "the parasitologist will be here in a
moment to remove you from society PLEASE have a candy!" penta-
gon cuts Iraqi circles square divide weapons contract by desire for
another Ramadan America's face the day money drifts out of reach
open your PDR Guide to Biological and Chemical Warfare Response
implement White House Crucifix Stool Softener the passion of
Chrissssssstina holds Papa's letter in air I leap hold on by my teeth I
may not have ovaries but I've planted my feet in this marsh more than
once Present? present our conscience to the world our sober apologies

(((((((((Pertho West
perforate the language bring no sleeping bag HEY does this mean we're
not staying? means there's no sleeping weigh your English Brother by
date and hour of atrocity weigh ourselves complicit with every
unanswered damnation my pop at cardboard box factory meditation
not preservation's sanity but sanity's preservation Philly sounds of
PhillySound now you take that P poets (!) sounding Philly young
palomino vegetarian in land of the cheese steak new plastic surgery
won't prevent new tumor (permanence is fiction's definition) Presley,
Lisa-Marie her father's face on blue balloon she carries to wood of
screaming crows "I'm glad you're all right!" yell it before waking

_____

i am
that is
awaiting your general duck shoot
i am
that is
not sure of the constructed mortal blind
i am
that is
open to suggestions for this pearl between my blades
i am
that is
not only going to tell them no but bake a pie of no
i am
that is
terror as laxative
i am
that is
winter in the guise of summer
i am
that is
hoping this brake brakes in time

dreamt they
forced my face
in Kafka's crotch
    it's amazing they
never noticed
i didn't resist

Kafka is dead
his penis
something
no one
knew

serious dream
is serious need
though i wouldn't
hurt a
monster

For Straight Guys
Who've Considered Suicide
When the K-Y Is Enough

are you worried I want you?
are you worried I jerk off
picturing you
naked
touching me?
swallowing me?
yeah
maybe I do
maybe I think about you
every night
and there's nothing you can do about it
and I tie you down
maybe you spread your ass cheeks
maybe you beg for more
and I smack you around
yeah
maybe I paint your nails
dress you in rubber
cuff you
drive you in your own car
places you never
wanted to go
maybe I push the car off a cliff
wave bye-bye as you scream at the back window
maybe I roll you in shit
take your pants off
let my horny german shepherd take a crack
maybe I've always
hated you more

maybe you had no idea
what an angry faggot
could do
yeah
maybe you ain't so good in bed
as you brag either
maybe you last a good 2
maybe 3 minutes
a bit too excited
runny nose
and all

POET-AGENT IN SEARCH OF TRANSVESTITE BOXER

The pink, frilly, faggy clip to the chin of oppression! While the fringe of the queer community is forgotten, even censored, we will make our way through the ranks all champion boxers made as an emblem for their minority outcast peoples throughout history! Looking for the world's toughest, queer transvestite boxer dedicated to winning the heavyweight belt. Must be willing to wear pink gloves with drawings of Judy Garland's face hitting the high note to punch out Tyson's woman-beating sorry ass once and for all! From there we will take the gay and lesbian community back from the money-sucking gay republican scum whose 1969 counterparts fled out the back door of Stonewall, leaving the revolution in the hands of the fearless queens and dykes! Can you resurrect queens as backbone of queer leadership? Do you make the high heeled, bitch hammer grade? Do you have Sissy Pride? Interested in victory? Contact CAConrad at (215)563-3075, or CAConrad13@AOL.com.

_____

above
anything
i value my
American
roots of
dissidence

maintenance of
removing control
off me control off
me control off me

commit the
muscle
to love

Philadelphia
doesn't mean
old British
settlement

servants
flip the
table

grab a
fly by its
little fly
liver

prepare for
the arsonists
of love
       got my
       ginger
ale and pretzel

smile not
dormant
on the
street

i'll be
arrested for
indecent
exposure if
i love this
city
more

c'mon
sweetheart!
let's run
away to
america
from here!

golden
piss we
make of
our piña
coladas

besides
it's the other
way around
we dont
kill time

"what is there to do in this city?" she asked, i said "this is Philadelphia it's Philadelphia i walk around touch things like trees and compose songs some call poems"

"but what is fun to do here?" she asked, i said "once someone on the other side of my wall turned to page 108 and i found myself on a street i forgot i loved...it was sublime"

i was on a game
show with
Marwan for gay
couples the game
show host was
this sexy nerd
who was a cross
between Paul
Blackburn and
Jerry Lewis it was
funny because
Marwan and i
were the only
couple NOT
arguing in fact we
laughed like we
used to the
audience thought
we were stoned
everything the
game show host
asked made us
BOTH think of
flowers beautiful
and blooming
Marwan pulled
this tight-budded
daisy from
nowhere he
whispered to it
till it slowly
opened to the
Oooh and Aaah
of us all

Leaving the Only Bed in America
That Keeps Me Satisfied

on the bus
i'm still in love with you
getting out of town
like you said
fast as i can
a flea
from your cat
works my ankle
chewing as much
as he can chew of me
and i'm wishing
he was
    so
     much
      big
       ger

I Still Have Keys to the Apartment

i let myself in
the new boyfriend
asleep with your arm
wrapped around his waist
looks like we did
i take my clothes off
to slide between you
but the cats fill my arms
i miss the cats because
they smell of you
i want to lick the hairs
on your chest flat
while the new boyfriend sleeps
but sniff the cats instead
i could feed my sperm
to your plants so part of me
would always be around
but you've swallowed
enough of me to feed
your bones and eyes that
you're not going
anywhere without me
i walk into the kitchen
careful to eat just one,
two grapes from the bunch
i hold back tears
see you still have
the smiling soccer ball
refrigerator magnets i gave you

the new boyfriend
doesn't know i bought them
i open the refrigerator
a little at a time
try to talk myself out of it
but open it anyway
i pee in the Pepsi
feel a little better
and grab my clothes
i want to leave the keys behind
but know i'll want
back in tomorrow

Weird without You

tired
of your circle
around me

tired
of the wait

tear a slot
in my side

feed your
loose
change

though
i'd give you
all i've got
for free

The Night River Phoenix Died

completely stoned
i'm having sex
with a man in a diner
against the restroom door
or was it against the
door to a dream since
no man could kiss
the way
i dream
his kiss
relaxed me
till i fell asleep
his tongue inside my
mouth a good two
minutes before
he heard me snore
he didn't take it well
didn't quite believe
it was the greatest
kiss of my life
i walked thru the diner
where the customers
and waitresses
knew where i had been
River Phoenix watched me
through the hole he'd chewed
in a piece of toast
i felt him read my thoughts
of walking on my knees to him

"forget it" he said "you
want to kiss me the way
i want to kiss James Dean
the kiss the dead kiss
would only put you to sleep"
"but those are my favorite kind" i said
and he slipped his tongue
through the hole in his toast
so i walked to his table
two feet shorter
on my knees

Regrets for Pussy:
A Revenge Spell

when he
left with her
i sewed a little
doll with his
face and pink
wooden cock

held it over
boiling water so he'd
strip naked along
the road

she thought it was
a party of course
and joined him

I'm so inspired
i whittle the cock its
sharpest while he's
driving into her

this little slut cried
wee wee wee

the coroner will
discover splinters of
flesh in her wounds

but no one
can identify the
pile of ash a
few feet away

Valentine's Day

you said cars
drive five
minutes
past the prison gate
before you
lose them
from your
cell

at three minutes
i stop to stare

each dark
window
you

Severed Leg Pirouette

"vacant land"
means no
people

"nothing but a few
prairie dogs"
means no
people

"we swerved, hit
a cat, but no one
was hurt"
means no
people

Fast Food Epiphany

my American Beef Consumption Average
met me at midnight
eating burgers in an empty parking lot
Heifer Spirits mooing in the back seat
i drive to McDonald's
do the Living Spirit Dance
around the deep fat fryer
around the spatula
prostrate before the grill
i chant apology
invoke the spirit COME!
someone calls the police
i dance again
someone screams
the Great Spirit Bull leaping over registers
charging tables with his horns
the Spirit Horse gallops from the freezer
(see who else we've eaten)
i ride the stallion thru the parking lot
my Great White Bellies
crush Lakota toddlers
i drive thru a store front
years of constipation
mess the silk of mannequins
fresh steaming excrement
a Sacred Cow porridge
i cake myself and howl
ancestors steering me
whirl me down the boulevard

sides of beef
circle overhead
quivering
into rigor mortis
the Spirit Herd
moos in harmony
follows me back
to pastures
the lot of us
dissolve into the
spinning top
of Saturn

she said shit should never come up in a poem
and i thought how shit always comes up with
me shit is life shit is always always always
coming out of you unless you're sick or
dead and dead is as good as shit to life
crawling with every possibility how did
shit get such a bad name why is shit
everybody's dirty little secret i know
you shit i look you in the eye am
listening to what you say but i'm
thinking you'll be taking a shit
sometime today she said
don't write about shit it's
awful it's disgusting
write about the
sunny day she
said write
about how
you feel
on this
sunny
day

Bran Muffins Have Nothing to Do with It! So There!

i defecated on a photo of myself as a child, so there!
i defecated on a photo of my mother
with her mouth open in surprise, so there!
i defecated on a bus and smeared it
on my reflection in the window, so there!
i defecated on a map of America
got forty-two states, so there!
i defecated on a globe with a light inside
until it couldn't shine anymore, so there!
i defecated on a picture of the Milky Way
in a *National Geographic* and it was sloppy, so there!
so there, so there, so there!
then i defecated on the bed sheets,
i sleep in my shit!
i spread it on toast in the morning! so there!
i walk, and no one loves me
'cause it's in my hair, it's in my eyes!
maybe they just can't see me beneath it
maybe they're shocked by a walking bowel movement
i don't know, but i don't care, so there!
but i can sure throw the dice beneath it
i can drink a milkshake and collect poems in it
i can nap in a bed of flowers till the rain comes

For Greg & Alison

bee in
flower
shop
makes
me feel
i'm back
on breast
milk

Celebrities I've Seen Offstage

Goober (what's his name?) from *The Gomer Pyle Show* on airplane to Chicago annoyed I didn't know who he was but I was only eleven his TV show before my time

Pope John Paul II outside St. Peter & Paul's cathedral our Catholic neighbor convinced my mother it would be educational for the kids to see him but truth was she just wanted a ride

Pete Rose signing autographs at the 1980 World Series in Vet Stadium I was wishing he was my father then I saw Tug McGraw and wished he was instead

Neil Diamond on Atlantic City boardwalk in blue western shirt smiling at the excitable young girls

Debbie Harry entering the Kennel Club I got high in an alley with my friends not old enough to get inside we imagined dancing and laughing doing lines of coke with Debbie singing "Heart of Glass" the higher we got

Allen Ginsberg reading "Sunflower Sutra" at the Painted Bride I jerked Barry off in the back row and later watched Ginsberg waste his angles on the straight boys

John Gotti stepping out of a South Philadelphia restaurant someone opened his car door for him I imagined the restaurant workers wiping their brows and relaxing

Melissa Etheridge in the lesbian bar after a concert my friend Kim ran upstairs to tell everyone but couldn't find her again when they came downstairs Kim made me tell them she wasn't making it up then Melissa walked out of the bathroom to a crowd of sighs

John Waters signing autographs Pegalina asked if she could bite his neck he agreed with a laugh which he soon regretted with a scream and asked us to leave we walked into The Rose Tattoo Pegalina announcing "I HAVE TASTED THE FLESH OF GENIUS!"

Tina Turner on Walnut Street her sweat evaporating and one day coming down again as rain turning into drinking water becoming us becoming her becoming us

Gregory Corso pacing back and forth in the North Star Bar office ranting at me, Janet, Jim and Dee about how we only wanted to open for him so we could ride his famous coattails which was crazy because we were invited to open for him he calmed down later and we all had a great night

Michael Moore at a book signing
    MOORE: (while signing my book) Where can I get a good
           cheese steak?
      ME: I'm a vegetarian
    MOORE: Oh, well *excuuuuuuuuuuuuuuuuse* me! NEXT! (to
           woman behind me) Where can I get a good cheese steak?
  WOMAN: I'm also a vegetarian
  MOORE: Why are ALL my fans vegetarians!?
      ME: We have problems with torture and murder for pleasure

Timothy Leary at Starwood having lunch the Reverend Velveteen Sly a couple of naked pagans asked if they could get their pictures taken on his lap he twitched his gray brow with a big smile happy to oblige

Annie Sprinkle was dating my friend Marie they came over for a tarot reading we spent most of the time talking about herbs to cure AIDS I don't remember if the tarot answered anyone that night

Henry Winkler on Benjamin Franklin Parkway annoyed me to think of jerking off as a kid "Oh Fonzie, cum on my FACE! SHOOT IT! SHOOT IT!" what was my deal back then?

The Frugal Gourmet shooting a segment of his cooking show in the Reading Terminal Market telling someone what a moron his cameraman was then oooing and aaahing over the pastries for the camera moments later

Pavarotti signing autographs for the crowd outside the Academy of Music seeing a plate of pasta with olive oil and broccoli rabe through the wall of the restaurant across the street with his superhero x-ray opera eyes

Howard Stern in Rittenhouse Square talking about "snapping gyro" with Jessica Hahn and Sam Kinnison after a show in the park heckling Philadelphia disc jockey John DiBella

Danbert Nobacon of Chumbawamba married my friend Kathy's daughter the three of them came over for a tarot reading Danbert sat on the couch not saying much while Kathy and Laura had a good time laughing with me on the floor reading the cards

Courtney Love and Billy Corrigan at J.C. Dobbs while I was on stage reading poems with Regie Cabico for the Lollapalooza show everyone lathered themselves in Courtney's drunken blond drama later she crossed the street to Zipperhead and set fire to T-shirts with Kurt's death certificate on them

Patti Smith outside the Trocadero a year later on South Street years later in HMV Records when she yelled at my friend Jeffery for taking her picture

Buffy Sainte-Marie being interviewed by PBS in museum making bullshit statements to the camera about how special and different artists are from "other people" when I told her my mother was a big fan she got annoyed because she's really caught in the same struggles as "other people" about aging

Quentin Crisp at a book signing
REPORTER: Quentin, how do you feel about chromosome testing to determine if an embryo is predisposed to being gay or lesbian to consider aborting the pregnancy?
CRISP: Sounds fine with me, my life has been miserable, I wouldn't wish it on anyone

I served Al Gore, Jimmy Carter and Nancy Reagan parmesan bread sticks at the Presidential Summit when I worked for Metropolitan Bakery their speeches on Welfare Reform infuriated me and the live gospel music made me want to shove a bread-stick up the ass of Christ to stop the music from celebrating the destruction of poor Americans and when skeletal Nancy creaked by I wanted to shout "MY FEET ARE SORE AND I CAN'T AFFORD TO GET SICK OR DIE YOU FUCKING BITCH!"

Laurie Anderson on Broad Street talking to a very sexy nerd with mustache very serious conversation serious and sexy seriously sexy

I served Oprah Winfrey a skinny mocha cappuccino and a low fat fruit bar when I worked at the Barnes & Noble cafe my coworker Paul cried when he told her how her show had saved his life and when she gave him a hug he wouldn't let go which was beautifully unnerving Oprah patting his back "Okay now...okay...okay...okay now"

Angela Davis at a book signing where a drag queen asked her why she had stayed in the closet so long I don't remember her answer the question much more interesting

Chastity Bono angry at my boss for running out of her book with C-SPAN and local news stations in the audience she told everyone to buy the book at Borders

Bruce Willis eating a sandwich on Pine Street taking a break from shooting *The Sixth Sense*

George and Barbara Bush campaigning for their son at the Republican Convention waving from the steps of the Union League I joined PETA oinking at them till George yelled something and a line of cops shoved us curbside

George W. Bush wincing and waving what's with the wincing? do I really care? no, just wondering if hair on his balls is also salt and pepper

SEXY Ralph Nader shaking hands during the 2000 presidential election I swear I could actually taste the man through the grip of his hand!

Andrew Tobias signing copies of his books *My Vast Fortune* and *The Best Little Boy in the World Grows Up*
    WOMAN: (whispers to me) He's so brave coming out of the closet
        ME: BRAVE!? It's 2001! While he was busy writing about
           his gay life under a pseudonym and making millions on
           the stock market from the other side of a closet door
           others were getting their heads bashed in fighting
           to make it safe for his rich white ass to FINALLY come
           out of the dark!

I sold a copy of *Gay & Lesbian Philadelphia* to John Waters

> WATERS: Is there a biography of Uncle Ed, you know, that crazy Philadelphia guy who bought young men's dirty socks and shitty underwear?
>
> ME: No, there isn't
>
> WATERS: Oh, what a shame, it's the ONLY biography I want to read!

SCRUMPTIOUS nerd Jeff Goldblum walking thru the Philip Guston show with beautiful blond she knows the taste of his cum *lucky lucky lucky* her!

Newt Gingrich in town for the World Affairs Council and he stops by the bookstore to sign his novel *Grant Comes East*

> CUSTOMER: I didn't know Washington types wrote novels
>
> ME: Washington hasn't been interested in nonfiction since the 1970s

Sold smiley Cameron Diaz a copy of *Philosophy for Dummies* and I thought to myself "THIS is going in my goddamned poem!"

keep
emailing Cher's website
"did i dream it or was there an
Andalusian rooster on *The Sony &*
Cher Comedy Hour strutting across stage
while you sang to a three year old
Chastity?" what's the big deal
why doesn't she get back
to me how hard
is it to
write
yes rooster
no rooster

my vending machine idea: tiny 50¢ fresco paintings turn our
lives around 50¢ of joy and pure hold them buy them frescoes vibrate
laid on your tongue ah man you never had it good as this them
frescoes timber me shivers a crack open sky of 50¢ don't you get it
don't you believe ah going to love you little ones

peering thru window
of Molly's bookshop
with Magdalena

stack of books
on counter

Baudelaire
under
biography of
Charlie Chaplin
(fine with me)
Simone de Beauvoir
on top of
them both
(even better)

Where Were You March 1st When a Great Poet Died?

at work being asked if
i'm rested up after trip to
New York as if time off
is   for   resting   up
refreshed   excited
running giddy back to
work work work work
WORK WORRRK!

(get fresh not
refreshed)

remember our dead fam-
ily of poets with an
appropriate degree of
rage but if you can't i've
got it covered don't
worry

(dream come join
another dream
John Wieners
no more
small shoes
of memory)

Pearl

Small pink glove on my grandmother's table. Did I hope it would be like holding her hand? Suddenly, like all spontaneous rituals somersault out of our skulls, I turn it inside out, saying the glove sends the soul Out...free.

Every closet I open, every bureau drawer, turn clothing inside out. Feels sure. And good. Walk outside, put my hands on the ice in her stone birdbath. As I burn it back to water a song waits on a branch overhead.

> You can't see her on this side anymore. You've got to sleep to find her. I'm in the middle of a large—I don't know—parking lot maybe. The rain is so hard I can't see through it but the umbrella is a good umbrella. Just stand there with the thought of walking but don't know where. She's not going to show herself. She's not ready. She's busy. They've got her doing things. I know I could throw the umbrella aside. It's warm rain. It's nice. But I've always hated water. I'll just crouch down in the middle of this, wait for the dream to end.

R.S.V.P.

he wrote "I have AIDS
and kissed this wall"
X marked the spot

I wrote "I'm not afraid"
and kissed him back
wherever he is

*"because it would be too stupid
finally
for so many to have died
and for you to live
without doing anything with your life."*
—Charlotte Delbo (poet who
survived Auschwitz)

_____

he's losing
weight you
better catch him

all frequencies
boss a
captured
thought behind
the eye

i'm always close
to the day i
loved him

love in custody
of time not
place close
to the day

don't say it
almost
say it

desert
in clay
pot moves
across
room in
his arms

evaporate again

i introduce the new hair
on my leg
to the rest of itself

we're so much
water we're clouds
when we die

i fill my mouth
on the rain
of your missing tongue

i will always drink from you

every year the night
Anne Sexton
killed herself
you said prayers
lit candles

i make space
between Neruda and Plath
where your book
could have been

water has no memory
of creating your thighs

the florist preferred
funerals over
weddings
though i preferred
to marry you

with just a touch
of lipstick
death disappears

on the street
our old friend Kit
called me your name
instead of mine

why do i still smell of you?

i tell you now
i lied sometimes
because i loved you

i dreamt
the downpour
of your hands
hung as icicles
from my window

i dreamt
colors you chose
each morning
sent my arms
one direction
or another

i dreamt
one pair of wings
between us
we leaned
in the sky

you said
hold your
hand out for my
weight tonight for what
falls from me

my hand cupped could
hold what's left of you

i walk to Topeka
in my sleep
your face on every
roadsign

puddles you reflected
evaporate again

sun trapped in
watermelon rinds i eat
lights my head at night

each morning
light knows seeds
under sidewalks
in the world you left behind

umbrellas fill the gunrack
where your picture
used to hang

old photograph of me

i remember his smile
behind the camera

———————

moths fly
at the
light
he put
in me

Brought tape recording of ocean tide to Atlantic City. Laid on beach, tape recorder at right ear, ocean at left. Eyes closed, I was between oceans, crash over here, crash over there. A brain takes the world at its word when spoken in water. Twice the tides matched, twice they entered me...together...synchro...

HOW A PLUNGE WENT THRU ME is the title of this at the end.

About the Author

CAConrad's childhood included selling cut flowers along the highway for his mother and helping her shoplift. He escaped to Philadelphia the first chance he got, where he lives and writes today with the PhillySound poets (www.phillysound.blogspot.com). He coedits *FREQUENCY Audio Journal* with Magdalena Zurawski, and edits the *9for9 project*. He has two forthcoming books, *The Frank Poems* (Jargon Society) and *advanced ELVIS course* (Buck Downs Books). He is the author of several chapbooks, including *(end-begin w/chants)*, a collaboration with Frank Sherlock. *Deviant Propulsion* is his first book.

Printed in the United States
By Bookmasters